If You Give A Girl A Push Up Bra

Written and Illustrated by
Miho Kahn

www.pushupbrabook.com
Copyright 2010 Miho Kahn
ISBN-13: 978-1461080299
ISBN-10: 1461080290
Digital design by Madelyn Snow
Additional copies may be ordered at: www.createspace.com

A Note From The Author:

I've always wanted to illustrate a children's book. I still hope to one day.

It's funny how our minds work, because even though *If You Give A Girl A Push-Up Bra* is not a children's book, it is inspired by one. Many of us remember the delightful book, *If You Give A Mouse A Cookie* by Laura Numeroff. The concept of consequences begetting consequences has lingered in my mind as my children have moved on from cookies to more adult themes.

If You Give A Girl A Push-Up Bra is my push-back against the onslaught of sexual imagery and messages that are foisted on our kids. At an age when they should still be enjoying the simplicity and awe of being a child, the world seduces them into adulthood— long before they are ready.

I hope you enjoy this book, and I hope you resist the lies.

My mother is a great artist. She is also a woman of few words. One day as I watched her painting she quietly said, "You have to be brave." I dedicate this book to my dearest Kahn and Kiya and I say to you as well, "Be Brave".

If you give a girl a push-up bra

She's going to like the way it makes her look.

She'll start wearing lots and lots of make-up

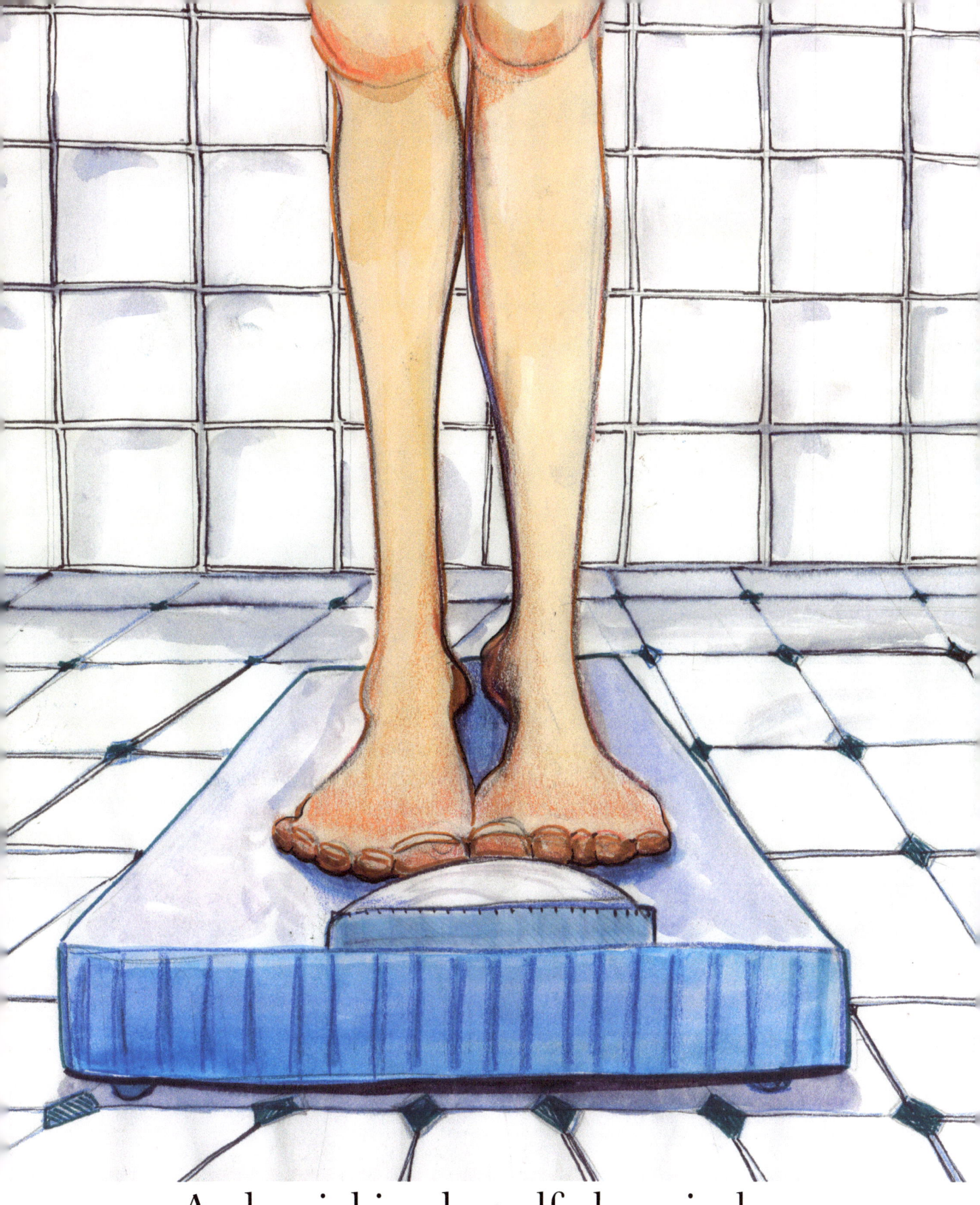

And weighing herself obsessively.

She'll buy lots of new clothes.

And find lots of new friends.

Eventually she'll meet a guy.

She won't know how to say "no" to him.

She'll go to a women's clinic for advice.

They will tell her that the pregnant tissue can be removed, but she will know that the tissue is really a baby.

She'll come home and tell you…

You'll convert the office to a nursery.

She'll miss the prom and be sad.

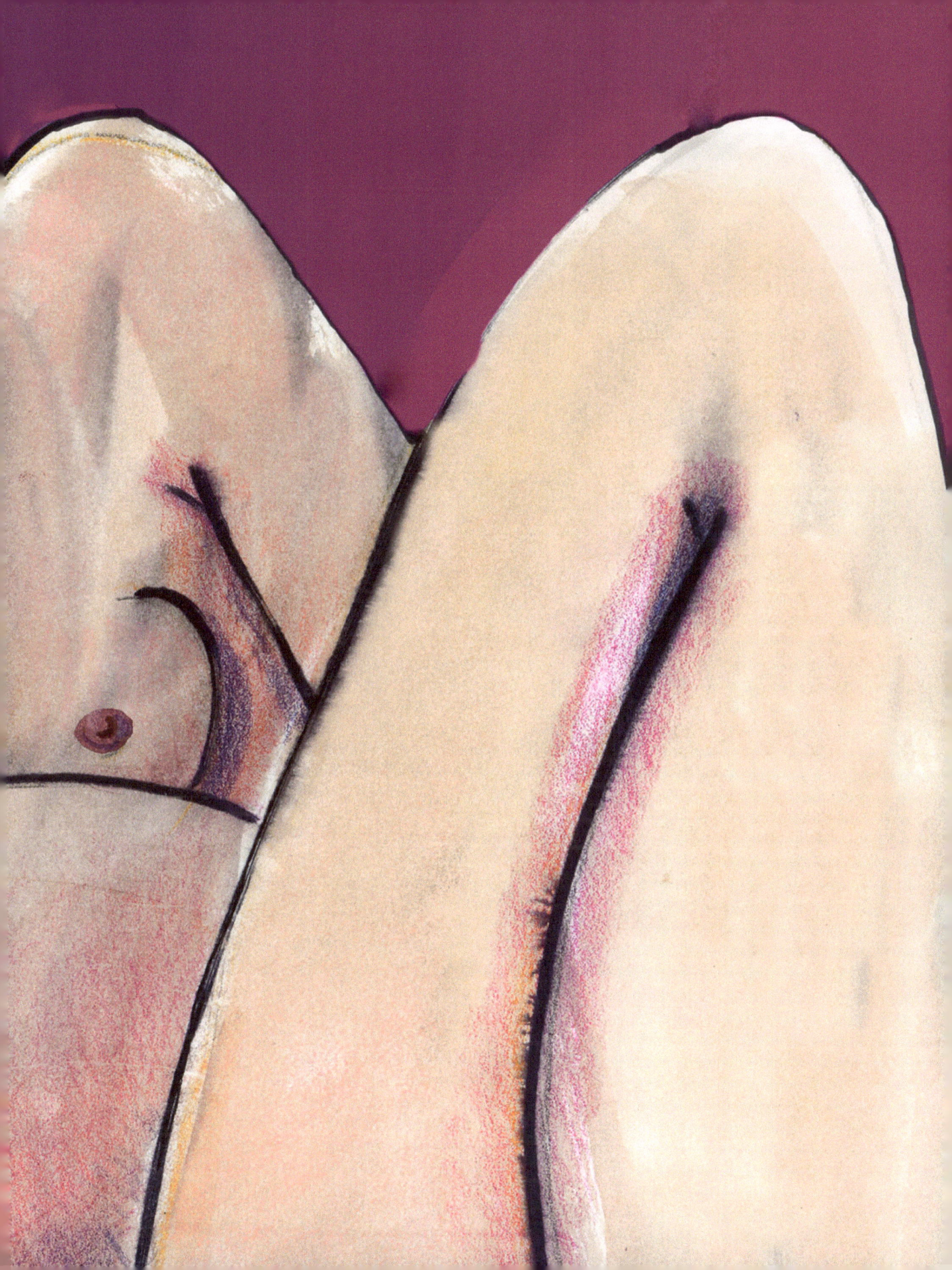

And after she's had the baby…

She'll need a push-up bra.

An Ongoing Conversation...

1. What do you think the girl is thinking about as she passes by the huge ad of the f a s h - ion model? Have you seen advertisements like that one? How did they make you feel?

2. How do you think the girl felt as she looked into the mirror while wearing her new bra? Did the bra make her feel different about herself? What kind of clothes might make you feel different about yourself? If she asked you how she looked in the bra, what would you tell her?

3. Why do you think she starts weighing herself? What happens when she looks at the scale? How do the numbers make her feel about herself? Does it matter to you what you weigh?

4. Why did the girl have trouble saying "no"?   Did she want to say no?

5. The girl gets pregnant and keeps the baby. What are some other options she might have considered? What are the advantages and disadvantages of each option? What do you think you would do?

6. How do you think her parents were affected?

7. What does "sexy" mean on TV or in magazines, movies, or videos? Why would commercials on TV suggest that young girls or boys be "sexy"?

8. At what age or point of development do you think a person should start dating? Start wearing makeup? Start kissing? Start having sex?

9. Why does she need a push-up bra after she's had the baby?

10. Does the girl seem different to you by the end of the book? How has she changed?

For more discussion questions and stuff to think about, go to:
www.pushupbrabook.com

About The Author

Miho Kahn is an interior designer who enjoys working in unusual spaces with adventurous clients. She paints, draws, sings, and gardens. Most recently Miho has been delighted and surprised to find herself performing a one-woman show that she wrote. Miho lives in Chester County, Pennsylvania with her husband, son, and daughter.

If you would like to see more of Miho's projects visit her websites at:
www.mihocleansheets.org and www.mihokahn.com

www.ingramcontent.com/pod-product-compliance
Lightning Source LLC
Chambersburg PA
CBHW041529280526
45792CB00004B/1433